MW01537838

THIS JOURNAL BELONGS TO:

Made in the USA
Monee, IL
30 September 2020

43618244R00056